EDITING AND PRODUCTION TEAM:

James F. Couch, Jr., Lyman Coleman, Sharon Penington, Cathy Tardif, Erika Tiepel, Katharine Harris, Scott Lee

SERENDIPITY
H O U S E

N A S H V I L L E , T E N N E S S E E

Published by Serendipity House Publishers
Nashville, Tennessee

International Standard Book Number: 1-57494-304-9

ACKNOWLEDGMENTS

Scripture quotations are taken from the Holman Christian Standard Bible,
© Copyright 2000 by Holman Bible Publishers. Used by permission.

06 07 08 / 10 9 8 7 6 5 4 3

Nashville, Tennessee
1-800-525-9563
www.serendipityhouse.com

WOMEN OF FAITH

GROUP DIRECTORY

Pass this Directory around and have your Group Members
fill in their names and phone numbers

Name

Phone

_____   _____

_____   _____

_____   _____

_____   _____

_____   _____

_____   _____

_____   _____

_____   _____

_____   _____

_____   _____

_____   _____

_____   _____

_____   _____

_____   _____

TABLE OF CONTENTS

CORE VALUES

Community: The purpose of this curriculum is to build community within the body of believers around Jesus Christ.

Group Process: To build community, the curriculum must be designed to take a group through a step-by-step process of sharing your story with one another.

Interactive Bible Study: To share your "story," the approach to Scripture in the curriculum needs to be open-ended and right brain—to "level the playing field" and encourage everyone to share.

Developmental Stages: To provide a healthy program throughout the four stages of the life cycle of a group, the curriculum needs to offer courses on three levels of commitment: (1) Beginner Level—low-level entry, high structure, to level the playing field; (2) Growth Level—deeper Bible study, flexible structure, to encourage group accountability; (3) Discipleship Level—in-depth Bible study, open structure, to move the group into high gear.

Target Audiences: To build community throughout the culture of the church, the curriculum needs to be flexible, adaptable and transferable into the structure of the average church.

Mission: To expand the Kingdom of God one person at a time by filling the "empty chair." (We add an extra chair to each group session to remind us of our mission.)

INTRODUCTION

Each healthy small group will move through various stages as it matures.

STAGE ONE

Birth Stage: This is the time in which group members form relationships and begin to develop community. The group will spend more time in ice-breaker exercises, relational Bible study and covenant building.

STAGE TWO

Growth Stage: Here the group begins to care for one another as it learns to apply what they learn through Bible study, worship and prayer.

STAGE FOUR

Multiply Stage: The group begins the multiplication process. Members pray about their involvement in new groups. The "new" groups begin the life cycle again with the Birth Stage.

STAGE THREE

Develop Stage: The inductive Bible study deepens while the group members discover and develop gifts and skills. The group explores ways to invite their neighbors and coworkers to group meetings.

 **Subgrouping:** If you have nine or more people at a meeting, Serendipity recommends you divide into subgroups of 3–6 for the Bible study. Ask one person to be the leader of each sub-group and to follow the directions for the Bible study. After 30 minutes, the Group Leader will call "time" and ask all subgroups to come together for the Caring Time.

Each group meeting should include all parts of the "three-part agenda."

Ice-Breaker: Fun, history-giving questions are designed to warm the group and to build understanding about the other group members. You can choose to use all of the Ice-Breaker questions, especially if there is a new group member that will need help in feeling comfortable with the group.

Bible Study: The heart of each meeting is the reading and examination of the Bible. The questions are open, discover questions that lead to further inquiry. Reference notes are provided to give everyone a "level playing field." The emphasis is on understanding what the Bible says and applying the truth to real life. The questions for each session build. There is always at least one "going deeper" question provided. You should always leave time for the last of the "questions for interaction." Should you choose, you can use the optional "going deeper" question to satisfy the desire for the challenging questions in groups that have been together for a while.

Caring Time: All study should point us to actions. Each session ends with prayer and direction in caring for the needs of the group members. You can choose between several questions. You should always pray for the "empty chair." Who do you know that could fill that void in your group?

SHARING YOUR STORY: These sessions are designed for members to share a little of their personal lives each time. Through a number of special techniques, each member is encouraged to move from low risk, less personal sharing to higher risk responses. This helps develop the sense of community and facilitates caregiving.

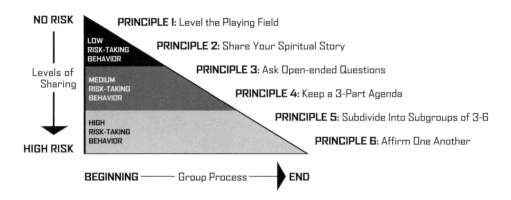

NO RISK

Levels of Sharing

HIGH RISK

LOW RISK-TAKING BEHAVIOR

MEDIUM RISK-TAKING BEHAVIOR

HIGH RISK-TAKING BEHAVIOR

PRINCIPLE 1: Level the Playing Field

PRINCIPLE 2: Share Your Spiritual Story

PRINCIPLE 3: Ask Open-ended Questions

PRINCIPLE 4: Keep a 3-Part Agenda

PRINCIPLE 5: Subdivide Into Subgroups of 3-6

PRINCIPLE 6: Affirm One Another

BEGINNING ——— Group Process ——▶ END

GROUP COVENANT: A group covenant is a "contract" that spells out your expectations and the ground rules for your group. It's very important that your group discuss these issues—preferably as part of the first session.

GROUND RULES:

- **Priority:** While you are in the group, you give the group meeting priority.

- **Participation:** Everyone participates and no one dominates.

- **Respect:** Everyone is given the right to their own opinion and all questions are encouraged and respected.

- **Confidentiality:** Anything that is said in the meeting is never repeated outside the meeting.

- **Empty Chair:** The group stays open to new people at every meeting.

- **Support:** Permission is given to call upon each other in time of need—even in the middle of the night.

- **Advice Giving:** Unsolicited advice is not allowed.

- **Mission:** We agree to do everything in our power to start a new group as our mission.

ISSUES:

- The time and place this group is going to meet is _____

- Refreshments are _____ responsibility.

- Child care is _____ responsibility.

Session 1

BEGINNING THE JOURNEY

Scripture Luke 5:1–11

Welcome to this study course for women seeking some encouragement along life's journey. In the following weeks, this group will focus on finding encouragement from these sources: (1) a caring group of women who will seek to support one another through prayer and friendship; (2) exploring the true stories of other women of faith and seeing how they faced challenges in their lives and how God upheld them; and (3) looking at God's Word and finding his direction to guide us on our journey of faith.

As with nearly every journey a person takes, the road can lead us through hills and valleys. Sometimes it may seem as if God has left us all alone. But the Bible gives us a far different message—God is one who acts on behalf of his people, to intervene for them and to care for them. God is acting all of the time. Some think God acts only on occasion through miracles. Scripture, however, tells us that God acts and is known through acts of nature (Rom. 1:19-20) and through the inner voice of conscience (1 Kings 19:12), as well as through various "signs and wonders" (John 2:23). God is constantly acting. By learning about how God has acted in the more distant past (through Bible study), and how he has acted in the more recent past (through listening to true stories of women of faith), we can more clearly see how God is acting and helping us on our journey today.

Ice-Breaker : 15 min.
CONNECT WITH YOUR GROUP

Leader

Be sure to read the introductory material in the front of this book prior to this first session. To help your group members get acquainted, have each person introduce herself and then take turns answering one or two of the Ice-Breaker questions. If time allows, you may want to discuss all three questions.

Today we are beginning our journey together as a group by talking about the beginning of the most important journey of all: the journey of faith. Before we start, take some time to get to know one another by sharing your responses to the following questions.

1. What do you think is the most perfect age, and why?

2. What is your favorite leisure time activity?
   ○ Reading.
   ○ Watching old movies.
   ○ Just spending some time with family or friends.
   ○ Playing games or sports.
   ○ Enjoying the outdoors.
   ○ What leisure time?
   ○ Other_____.

3. What do you consider to be your greatest accomplishment?

 Study Time: 30 min.
READ ÷ DISCUSS

Leader

The Study in these sessions is in two parts: the first is a Life Story Illustration of an incident in the life of a great woman of faith; the second is a study of Scripture. Select two members of the group ahead of time to read aloud the Life Story and the Scripture passage. Then discuss the Questions for Interaction that follow. Be sure to save time at the end for the Caring Time.

LIFE STORY ILLUSTRATION

Called to Faith

Patricia St. John is best known to us today as the beloved author of many children's books, including *Treasures of the Snow* and *The Tanglewood's Secret*. She grew up in a happy and lively household, with parents who loved the Lord and she first heard the call of the Lord as a little girl. In her autobiography, *An Ordinary Woman's Extraordinary Faith,* she recounts the story of one evening's reading time. Her mother had read a story that contained a verse from Isaiah 43, and had her children learn it by heart: "Thus saith the Lord, fear not; I have redeemed thee, I have called thee by thy name; thou art mine."

"I, probably aged about six, did not understand the word redeemed but the last two phrases seemed clear and simple. I went straight up to the room where we slept and I knelt down. 'My name is Patricia,' I said, 'and if you are really calling me I want to come and be yours.'

"I cannot remember any clear result except that, next morning I ran out into the garden and looked up into the hollyhocks, which were much taller than I was, and thought how exquisitely beautiful they were. It is my first memory of consciously noticing beauty and surely this was to have been expected. I had, in a new way become God's child; I had been accepted into the realm of beauty."

Patricia continued to grow in the midst of her busy, cheerful family and along with the interesting life of their home with its constant stream of visitors, she had what she called her "almost secret world" of the hills and fields around their country home. The beauties of nature had a strong pull for her, for, as she said, "Something happened in my early teens that somehow changed the face of nature. I was at that stage a headstrong child, prone at times to tempers and sulks and I hated myself. I loved my home and my family and no child could have longed more to be helpful and admired. I remember waking, morning after morning, resolving that today at least, I would be that little ray of sunshine—only to fail miserably the first time my will was crossed. I told no one, but I was gradually sinking into mystified despair; why, oh why, could I not be what I longed to be?

"Then one day after some angry outburst, I went to my room and picked up that old Bible that I had almost ceased to read and I opened it at Revelation 3:20 which I must have known by heart for many years. But that day I seemed to understand the words for the first time: 'Behold I stand at the door and knock; if any man hear my voice and open the door, I will come in.' I seemed to see not a closed door, but a little ship, tossed out of course by winds and waves, with no hope of ever reaching the harbor. And I seemed to see Jesus standing in the storm and saying, 'If you will ask me in I will take you where you want to go.' I think I cried out aloud, 'Oh please, please come in.'

"Since that first, long-ago child's grasp of Isaiah 43:1, I had never doubted that I belonged to the Lord, and this in no way negated that experience. To receive is simply a further step to belonging. It just confirmed what was once said by a well-known children's evangelist, 'A little child needs a little child's Savior. A growing child needs a growing child's Savior.' Over and over, in each stage of our growth he reveals himself in the very way that we need him.

"I don't think there was any great outward difference. I was still prone, at times, to the traumas of a self-willed, emotional teenager, but inwardly something had changed. I knew he was there, part of me, and I knew that there was hope, and that if I remembered to call out to him, he could control me. But more than that, the world had changed. I had always loved growing things, but now it was his life springing up; I had always loved light—sunrise, clouds and sunset, but now he was that light."[1]

SCRIPTURE PASSAGE

Responding to the call to follow Jesus is the first step on the journey of faith. Read Luke 5:1–11 and think about what it means to follow that call.

Jesus Calls the First Disciples

5 *As the crowd was pressing in on Jesus to hear God's word, He was standing by Lake Gennesaret. ²He saw two boats at the edge of the lake; the fishermen had left them and were washing their nets. ³He got into one of the boats, which belonged to Simon, and asked him to put out a little from the land. Then He sat down and was teaching the crowds from the boat.*

⁴When He had finished speaking, He said to Simon, "Put out into deep water and let down your nets for a catch."

5"Master," Simon replied, "we've worked hard all night long and caught nothing! But at Your word, I'll let down the nets."

*6*When they did this, they caught a great number of fish, and their nets began to tear. *7*So they signaled to their partners in the other boat to come and help them; they came and filled both boats so full that they began to sink.

*8*When Simon Peter saw this, he fell at Jesus' knees and said, "Depart from me, because I'm a sinful man, Lord!" *9*For he and all those with him were amazed at the catch of fish they took, *10*and so were James and John, Zebedee's sons, who were Simon's partners.

"Don't be afraid," Jesus told Simon. "From now on you will be catching people!" *11*Then they brought the boats to land, left everything, and followed Him.

Luke 5:1–11

 # QUESTIONS FOR INTERACTION

Leader
Be sure to read the Summary and Study Notes at the conclusion of this session and refer to these during the discussion as needed. If 30 minutes is not enough time to answer all of the questions in this section, conclude the Bible Study by answering question 7.

1. When you were a teenager, whom did you admire most? What did you admire about this person? How would you have reacted if that person had asked you to become a personal friend?

2. If you had been in Simon's shoes when Jesus asked him to let down his nets, how would you have responded?

3. In what ways can you relate to Patricia's story of the call to follow Jesus? In what ways can you relate to the story of how Simon, Andrew and Zebedee's sons became disciples?

4. When did you first hear the "call" to begin your spiritual journey? Did you respond right away? Share with the group a little about the beginning of your faith journey.

5. In comparison to the fishermen, where are you right now in your spiritual journey?
   ○ Like Simon, ready to do what Jesus says even if I don't understand it.
   ○ Afraid of what might be ahead.
   ○ Seeing myself as unworthy to follow Jesus.
   ○ Sinking, like the boat full of fish—I'm getting too much all at once.
   ○ Dropping everything to follow him.
   ○ I'm not sure what he wants from me.

6. What does it mean to "leave everything and follow him" today? How close have you come to doing this?

7. What does your next step need to be in your spiritual journey?

GOING DEEPER:

If your group has time and/or wants a challenge, go on to this question.

8. Why does Peter respond to the huge catch of fish the way he does in verse 8? Have you ever looked at yourself in this light? What did you see?

Caring Time : 15 min.
APPLY THE LESSON AND PRAY FOR ONE ANOTHER

Leader

Take some extra time in this first session to go over the introductory material at the beginning of this book. At the close, pass around your books and have everyone sign the Group Directory.

This very important time is for developing and expressing your concern for each other as group members by praying for one another.

1. Agree on the group covenant and ground rules found in the introductory pages.

2. Begin the prayer time by taking turns sharing a specific praise or problem that the group can pray for.

3. Pray specifically for God to lead you to someone to bring next week to fill the empty chair.

NEXT WEEK

In this week's session we focused on beginnings—not only the beginning of this group, but more importantly the beginning of our own journey of faith. It is encouraging to look back on this and realize that God has had his hand on us far longer than we even realized it. During the coming week, take a little time each day to pray and ask God to show you the next step on this important journey. Next week we will consider how God has promised us the Holy Spirit to help us on our journey.

NOTES ON LUKE 5:1–11

Summary: All four of these fishermen had probably at least seen Jesus around and were familiar with who he was. When the crowd began to press too close, Jesus asked Simon to take him out a little way in his boat. Sound travels well over water, and this way the people in the back of the crowd had a better chance of hearing. Simon made no objection to lending his boat, but he couldn't help protesting when Jesus asked him to do a seemingly silly thing. Nevertheless, he agreed to do it anyway, and their fruitless night was suddenly made up for. It must have been startling to say the least. In the other gospel accounts, Jesus specifically says, "follow me," but Luke does not mention this. Instead he focuses on Simon's realization of his own sinfulness, and Jesus' rather unusual response: "Don't be afraid ... from now on you will be catching people!"

5:1 Lake Gennesaret. This is another name for the Sea of Galilee.

5:2 washing their nets. In the morning, fishermen would clean and repair their nets, which they dragged along behind the boats while fishing through the night.

5:3 the boats. While one belonged to Simon, the other boat may have been owned by James and John (Mark 1:19), Simon's partners in the fishing business (v. 10). These would have been open craft about 20 to 30 feet long.

5:4–5 From any normal perspective, Jesus' command was absolutely foolish since mid-morning was not the time fish would be feeding. To get the feeling behind the words in verse 5, one must picture tired and hungry men who have worked unsuccessfully all night suddenly wondering why in the world they should listen to a religious teacher when it comes to their fishing business! Still, Simon Peter decides to go along with him and is rewarded for it.

5:6–7 In contrast to Simon's doubt, Luke underscores the magnitude of the catch. It was so large that it tore the nets and threatened to sink Simon's boat as well as that of his partners!

5:8 Simon Peter's fear and confession before Jesus is similar to that of people in the Old Testament when they encountered the divine (1:12,29; 2:9; Isa. 6:5; Dan. 10:15). In particular, like with Isaiah, encountering divine power caused Simon Peter to focus on his awareness of his own sinfulness. In Isaiah's case, God responded by sending an angel to "cleanse" him with a burning coal. Then, as with Simon Peter, God then gave Isaiah a mission (Isa. 6:8). Just what Simon Peter recognized about Jesus' identity at this point is unclear since "Lord" can be a title for God or a title of respect for an esteemed person. In any case, it is apparent that Simon Peter was thoroughly convinced that Jesus was at least a rabbi who was more interesting than most.

5:10 Don't be afraid. Jesus' words echo those of the divine response seen in Isaiah 6, Daniel 10 and elsewhere. **you will be catching people.** The climax of the story is not Jesus' self-revelation, but its significance as a graphic illustration of the certain widespread success that would accompany Simon Peter's (and the other apostles') mission of preaching the kingdom of God (4:43). Whereas fish are caught, to their own detriment, for the advantage of another (those who will eat them), people are "caught" for their own benefit— that they might realize the fullness of God's love and forgiveness.

5:11 they ... left everything, and followed Him. A loyalty to Jesus that takes precedence over anything else in life is Luke's characteristic way of describing what it means to be a follower of Christ.

[1]Patricia St. John, *An Ordinary Woman's Extraordinary Faith* (Wheaton, IL: Harold Shaw Publishers, 1993), pp. 37, 53-55.

Session 2

HELP FOR THE JOURNEY

Scripture **John 14:15–21, 25–27**

LAST WEEK

In last week's session, we started this study course by talking about beginnings, especially spiritual beginnings. We spent some time exploring the idea of God calling people to follow him, and shared from our own lives how we first heard the "call" to begin our own journeys of faith. This week we will look together at one of the most encouraging promises God has given us: we will never be alone because we have unfailing help and direction for our journey through his gift of the Holy Spirit.

Ice-Breaker : 15 min.
CONNECT WITH YOUR GROUP

Leader

Begin the session with a word of prayer. Have your group members take turns sharing their responses to one, two or all three of the Ice-Breaker questions. Be sure everyone gets a chance to participate.

Our lives are full of directions of different kinds, everything from traffic signals to well-meaning advice from friends. Sometimes there are so many it is hard to know which way to turn.

Before we go on to our study of the real director of our lives, take some time to get to know one another better as you answer the following questions.

1. How are you at following instructions when you put something together?
    ○ I only read them when everything else fails.
    ○ They make me feel rebellious.
    ○ I memorize all ten pages before I even take the parts out of the box.
    ○ You mean this thing actually came with instructions?
    ○ I think instructions squelch creativity, so I ignore them.

2. If you were to select a traffic sign to describe how you've been living your life, what sign would it be?

   ○ Merge: I've been trying to get along with everyone.

   ○ Keep Right: I'm trying to stay on the right track.

   ○ One Way: I am seeking to be more decisive in my life direction.

   ○ Yield: I'm seeking to yield my life to God.

   ○ Under Construction: I'm changing so much.

   ○ Do Not Enter: I'm having a hard time looking at my past or at who I really am.

3. When have you felt the most alone? How did you handle the situation?

 | ## Study Time: 30 min.
READ ÷ DISCUSS

Leader
Have two members of the group, selected ahead of time, read aloud the Life Story and the Scripture passage. Then discuss the Questions for Interaction that follow. Be sure to save time at the end for the Caring Time.

LIFE STORY ILLUSTRATION

The Presence of the Spirit

Corrie ten Boom and her family sheltered Jews from the Nazis in Holland during World War II. Eventually, they were caught and she and her sister Betsie were sent to one of the infamous Nazi concentration camps. In her book, *Tramp for the Lord*, she tells of the comfort of the Holy Spirit even in the midst of what we would call hell on earth.

"As a little girl, Corrie and her cousin Dot liked to play in the old church near her home. Corrie's uncle was the caretaker, and the children loved the old building.

"One afternoon we played very late, and before we knew it, the darkness of the cathedral swallowed us up. I looked around. Through the beautiful stained glass windows I saw a little light coming in from the streets around. Only the silhouettes of the Gothic pillars stood out in the darkness as they reached upward and upward.

" 'Let's go home,' whispered Dot. 'I'm scared.'

"I was not. Slowly I went to the usher's door that opened out to where Uncle Arnold lived. There was a Presence that comforted me, a deep peace in my heart. Even in the darkness, smelling the dust and dampness of the church building, I knew that the 'Light of the World' was present. Was the Lord preparing me for some time in the future when I would need to know that His light is victorious over all darkness?

"It was forty-five years later. Betsie and I walked to the square where roll call was being held in the concentration camp. It was still early, before dawn. The head of our barracks was so cruel that she had sent us out into the very cold outdoors a full hour too early.

"Betsie's hand was in mine. We went to the square by a different way from the rest of our barracks-mates. We were three as we walked with the Lord and talked with Him. Betsie spoke. Then I talked. Then the Lord spoke. How? I do not know. But both of us understood. It was the same Presence I had felt years before in the old cathedral in Haarlem.

"The brilliant early morning stars were our only light. The cold winter air was so clear. We could faintly see the outlines of the barracks, the crematorium, the gas chamber, and the towers where the guards were standing with loaded machine guns.

" 'Isn't this a bit of heaven!' Betsie had said. 'And Lord, this is a small foretaste. One day we will see You face-to-face, but thank You that even now You are giving us the joy of walking and talking with You.'

"Heaven in the midst of hell. Light in the midst of darkness. What a security!"[1]

SCRIPTURE PASSAGE

While Jesus was ministering on this earth, his followers had great security in knowing that he was there to tell them what to do. But when he was preparing to leave this life for the next, he had to point them to a source of direction that would stay with them. Otherwise, when they came to divergent paths, how would they know the way? Christ's answer to this was to point them to an "internal compass." He would give them the Holy Spirit who would be within them. Jesus had been an external compass, and that which is external can always be taken away. Some people try the external compass of a strong-willed person's opinions. Sometimes this might be a pastor, or a parent, or a friend. But whoever it is, an external guide can be taken away. Read John 14:15–21,25-27 and take comfort in Jesus' promise of an internal compass can never be taken away.

Jesus Promises the Holy Spirit

[15]"If you love Me, you will keep My commandments. [16]And I will ask the Father, and He will give you another Counselor to be with you forever. [17]He is the Spirit of truth, whom the world is unable to receive because it doesn't see Him or know Him. But you do know Him, because He remains with you and will be in you. [18]I will not leave you as orphans; I am coming to you.

[19]"In a little while the world will see Me no longer, but you will see Me. Because I live, you will live too. [20]In that day you will know that I am in My Father, you are in Me, and I am in you. [21]The one who has My commandments and keeps them is the one who loves Me. And the one who loves Me will be loved by My Father. I also will love him and will reveal Myself to him." ...

[25]"I have spoken these things to you while I remain with you. [26]But the Counselor, the Holy Spirit, whom the Father will send in My name, will teach you all things and remind you of everything I have told you.

[27]"Peace I leave with you. My peace I give to you. I do not give to you as the world gives. Your heart must not be troubled or fearful.

John 14:15–21,25–27

? | QUESTIONS FOR INTERACTION

Leader

If you have more than seven or eight women in your group, divide into sub-groups of three to six to discuss the Questions for Interaction. Refer to the Summary and Study Notes at the end of this session as needed. If 30 minutes is not enough time to answer all of the questions in this section, conclude by answering question 7.

1. Who was the best counselor you ever had? Why was this person so special?

2. In your search for spiritual direction, what is most likely to divert you from the path?
   ○ My desire for money and nice things.
   ○ My desire to be a "people-pleaser."
   ○ My own stubbornness.
   ○ My desire to achieve and find recognition for my accomplishments.
   ○ Being too busy with day-to-day life to find time for it.
   ○ Other_____.

3. How would you describe your personal relationship with Jesus right now?
   ○ I feel like an orphan.
   ○ We talk now and then.
   ○ We are getting acquainted.
   ○ We have a close relationship.
   ○ Other_____.

4. What is the closest you have come to experiencing the presence of God as Corrie and Betsie did in the prison camp?

5. What is the Holy Spirit's purpose in our lives? What does it mean to be in Jesus, or to have him in us (v. 20)?

6. What is the relationship between obedience and love? How does this work out in your life?

7. Of all the promises made in this Scripture passage, which one means the most to you? Why?

GOING DEEPER:

If your group has time and/or wants a challenge, go on to this question.

8. For what do you most need the Holy Spirit's counsel in your life right now? What do you need to do to be better able to receive the Holy Spirit's direction?

Caring Time : 15 min.

APPLY THE LESSON AND PRAY FOR ONE ANOTHER

Leader
Bring the group members back together and begin the Caring Time by sharing responses to all three questions. Be sure to take turns so everyone gets a chance to participate, and don't forget to pray for someone to fill the empty chair.

Take time now to share how God is working in your lives and to pray for and support one another.

1. Have you ever felt orphaned, either literally or figuratively? What made you feel this way? In what way could this week's study comfort you?

2. How satisfied do you feel with the level of your relationship with Jesus? How can this group pray for you as you seek to know him better?

3. Is there something you would especially like to thank God for this week?

P. S. Add new group members to the Group Directory at the front of this book.

NEXT WEEK

In today's session, we discussed Jesus' promise to send the Holy Spirit, and talked about what this means in our lives. We also read a true life story of two women who experienced the real presence of this same Spirit in the midst of one of the most difficult circumstances we can imagine. Take a few moments each day in the coming week, and thank God for his gift of the Holy Spirit to comfort and guide us on our journey. Next week we will be looking at another passage in the book of John that brings us another encouraging message: God is protecting and looking after us.

NOTES ON JOHN 14:15–21,25–27

Summary: This passage from John's gospel is part of a long discourse Jesus had with his disciples at the Last Supper, preparing them for his imminent death, resurrection and ascension to the Father. The promise of the coming Holy Spirit is given after he has told them the hard truths of his betrayal and predicted Peter's denial. He goes on to give them hope and comfort, not only of the joys to come when they would be reunited in heaven, but also that he would not leave them alone or without aid until that time. The Counselor sent from the Father will be with believers forever, as a guide and for comfort. Jesus also emphasizes the relationship between love for him and obedience in the Christian's life. Finally, he tells them that he is also giving them his peace and urges them not to be afraid.

14:16 another Counselor. The Greek term *paraclete* is a rich term for which there is no sufficient English translation. Attempts such as "Counselor" or "Helper" or "Comforter" fail because they emphasize only one of many aspects of the term. Since this discourse presents the ministry of the Spirit in the same terms as that of Jesus, the Spirit can be referred to as another *"Paraclete"* like Jesus (1 John 2:1).

14:17 the world is unable to receive. Just as the "world" has not accepted Jesus, nor the Father (5:37–38), neither will it be able to receive the Spirit. **He remains with you and will be in you.** This parallelism does not create distinctions between "with" and "in," but simply adds emphasis to Jesus' dramatic announcement. The reality of the indwelling Spirit lifts the Old Testament expectation of a new covenant, wherein God would dwell with his people, to unimaginable heights (Isa. 7:14; Jer. 31:31–34; Ezek. 34:30). It is this indwelling of the Spirit with God's people that ultimately makes the temple and the issue of where to worship irrelevant (4:21).

14:18 I will not leave you as orphans. When a rabbi died, his disciples were spoken of as being orphaned. **I am coming to you.** In this context, the coming of Jesus spoken of here should be understood in terms of the coming of the Spirit. It is in that way that they will "see" him, whereas the world will not (v. 19).

14:20 In that day. This speaks of the time when the Spirit will be given to the disciples. **I am in My Father, you are in Me, and I am in you.** The intimate relationship Jesus enjoys with the Father is the pattern for the relationship believers will enjoy with him. Since in verse 17 he said the Spirit will be in believers, this verse establishes the shared identity of the Spirit and Jesus.

14:21 reveal Myself to him. This too is related to the coming of the Spirit. Just as the person who has seen Jesus has "seen" the Father (v. 19), so the one who has been given the Spirit has "seen" Jesus.

14:26 whom the Father will send. Here and in verse 16 it is the Father who sends the Spirit to the believer. In 15:26 and 16:7, Jesus says he will send the Spirit. **will teach you ... and remind you.** These parallel verbs are two ways of saying the same thing. The purpose of the teaching of the Spirit is not to impart new information, but to remind believers of the truth Jesus taught and help them apply it to ever-changing situations.

14:27 Peace. Although this was a common expression used upon meeting or leaving someone, in this gospel it is a catchword that sums up all Jesus will provide for his people (16:33; 20:19,21, 26). The word is used in the same way in Isaiah 9:7; 52:7 and 54:10 to speak of the blessings God will give to his people in the days of the Messiah. In Ezekiel 37:26, God calls the covenant that he will establish with his people a "covenant of peace." Jesus is instituting this covenant here.

---

[1]Corrie ten Boom, *Tramp for the Lord* (Fort Washington, PA: Christian Literature Crusade; Old Tappan, NJ: Fleming H. Revell Company, 1974), pp. 29-30.

Session 3

PROTECTION FOR THE JOURNEY

Scripture **John 10:11–18**

 ## LAST WEEK

Last week we were encouraged as we looked at the special promise Jesus gave his disciples to send the Holy Spirit to help them. We saw how he kept his promise many years later to two women in a concentration camp, and talked about how that promise affects our own lives. This week we will find another source of strength and courage as we realize that God is our Protector.

 ## Ice-Breaker : 15 min.
CONNECT WITH YOUR GROUP

Leader
Choose one or two of the Ice-Breaker questions. If you have a new group member you may want to do all three. Remember to stick closely to the three-part agenda and the time allowed for each segment.

Fear and feelings of insecurity are things we all deal with at some point in our lives, even when we appear to "have it made." Take some time now to get to know each other better as you share from your own unique life experiences with fearfulness.

1. When you were a child, what were you most afraid of?
   ○ The dark.
   ○ A mean teacher.
   ○ The school or neighborhood bully.
   ○ Fires.
   ○ Nightmares.
   ○ Other_____.

2. Who was the most comforting to you when you were afraid?

3. Do you like to watch scary movies now, or do you hide your head under a pillow when the suspense music begins?

Study Time: 30 min.
READ ÷ DISCUSS

Leader
Choose two members of the group ahead of time to read aloud the Life Story and the Scripture passage. Then discuss the Questions for Interaction, breaking up into smaller groups as necessary.

LIFE STORY ILLUSTRATION

Those People in White

Darlene Deibler Rose and her husband, Russell Deibler, went as pioneer missionaries to open the interior of Dutch New Guinea in the late thirties. When the Japanese occupied the area during World War II, Darlene and several other women were left with an older missionary couple as their husbands were trucked off to prison camps. In her autobiography, *Evidence Not Seen*, Darlene tells the story of one time when they experienced God's protection in a dramatic way.

With the tremendous unrest in the community, they knew that a household of women and one old man would be particularly vulnerable to attacks by bandits and looters. Late one night Darlene heard a scrabbling noise in the living room of the house, and thinking that it was another invasion of the rats they had been fighting for the last weeks, she called her friend and got up to chase them out so they could get some sleep. As she opened the door, she thought she saw something swish by her.

"When I stepped out into the hall to get a better look, I found myself face to face with a Boegis bandit. He was wearing a black sarong that he had swooped up over his shoulder to free his machete. With one fluid movement, the knife was extricated from his belt and held up in striking position. I'm really quite a coward, and why I rushed at him, I have no idea. Perhaps it was the element of surprise, but he was a bigger coward than I, for he turned and fled down the hall, through the bathroom, across the porch, and down over the mountainside with me hot on his heels—until I saw others emerge from the jungle. He yelled something in their language, and together they fled. I stopped dead. 'Lord,' I whispered, 'what a stupid thing for me to do!'

"Immediately he answered, 'The angel of the Lord encampeth round about them that fear Him, and delivereth them.'...

"Dr. and Mrs. Jaffray were now awake and had joined Margaret. 'What happened?' Dr. Jaffray asked, much shaken by the noise and the sight of the damaged door.

" 'We had bandits! They must have been here for hours. I thought they were rats!' A tour of inspection proved that tablecloths and other linens were missing, books had been pulled from the shelves and searched, probably by someone expecting to find money in them—and I had thought they were rats! ...

"From that night on, we slept with a club at the foot of our bed and a small milk can-squawker under our pillows, but we never had to use them. We heard bandits return several nights after that, but they never again entered the house. It wasn't until after the war that I learned why. I had suspected the Jaffray's gardener; he was Boegis, and he knew the layout of the house. When I asked him why they never entered the house again, he answered incredulously, 'Because of those people you had there—those people in white who stood about the house.' The Lord had put His angels around us. He had delivered."[1]

SCRIPTURE PASSAGE

So far we have been encouraged by knowing that God provides help and direction as we travel along on the winding path of life. Along this path, we may find danger lurking in the shadows, and sometimes our fears can become a reality. Read John 10:11–18 and be cheered as you listen to God's promise of his protection for our eternal well-being.

The Good Shepherd

[11]"I am the good shepherd. The good shepherd lays down his life for the sheep. [12]The hired man, since he's not the shepherd and doesn't own the sheep, leaves them and runs away when he sees a wolf coming. The wolf then snatches and scatters them. [13]This happens because he is a hired man and doesn't care about the sheep.

[14]"I am the good shepherd. I know My own sheep, and they know Me, [15]as the Father knows Me, and I know the Father. I lay down My life for the sheep. [16]But I have other sheep that are not of this fold; I must bring them also, and they will listen to My voice. Then there will be one flock, one shepherd. [17]This is why the Father loves Me, because I am laying down My life that I may take it up again. [18]No one takes it from Me, but I lay it down on My own. I have the right to lay it down, and I have the right to take it up again. I have received this command from My Father."

John 10:11–18

 # QUESTIONS FOR INTERACTION

Leader

Refer to the Summary and Study Notes at the conclusion of this session as needed. If 30 minutes is not enough time to answer all of the questions in this section, conclude the Bible Study by answering question 7.

1. What do you know about shepherds? What does this metaphor say to you? Can you think of a similar example of a good caregiver who has been important in your life?

2. What "wolf" threatens you most at this point in your life?
   ○ Financial stress.
   ○ Family stress.
   ○ Job stress.
   ○ Health problems.
   ○ Isolation and loneliness.
   ○ Reoccurring temptation.
   ○ Other_____.

3. What stands out to you the most in this passage? Why?

4. What is Jesus saying about the kind of help he offers to those who would follow him?
   ○ He'll protect us from all danger.
   ○ Whatever we face, he'll stand with us.
   ○ Following his voice will help keep us out of trouble.
   ○ He'll protect us from the sting of death by his own death and resurrection.
   ○ Other_____.

5. What is the biggest difference between the hired hand and the shepherd? What is the response of the "sheep" to the shepherd who desires to do so much for them?

6. Who are the "other sheep" he must bring also (vv. 17–18)? What characterizes his flock?

7. How can you discern the Good Shepherd's voice from all the voices that compete for your attention? How can you become so familiar with his voice that you know him when he speaks to you?

 ## GOING DEEPER:
If your group has time and/or wants a challenge, go on to this question.

---

8. The protection Darlene and her friends received from God was physical protection from a specific danger. It is encouraging to know that God can and does protect from such danger. But later on, God allowed Darlene to go through some experiences that seem far more terrible than being robbed. How does this fit with the image of the Good Shepherd who protects his flock from the wolves?

Caring Time : 15 min.
APPLY THE LESSON AND PRAY FOR ONE ANOTHER

Leader
Begin the Caring time by having group members take turns sharing responses to all three questions. Be sure to save at least the last five minutes for a time of group prayer. Remember to include a prayer for the empty chair when concluding the prayer time.

One of the important sources of encouragement that God has planned for us is fellowship with caring friends. Devote this time now to listening to one another and praying for one another's specific concerns.

1. How comfortable do you feel sharing your needs and struggles with this group? What would make it easier for you?

2. Where do you need God's protection in your life right now? How can this group pray for you as you deal with the "wolves" you mentioned in question 2 of the study time?

3. Do you have a particular praise or prayer need you would like to share with the group today?

NEXT WEEK

In this week's session, we explored Jesus as the Good Shepherd who knows, loves and protects believers as his "sheep." We read a true story of a group of women who experienced this protective care in a dramatic way when they were threatened by bandits. But we also learned that the protection of our Good Shepherd goes far beyond the physical body. He loved us enough to lay down his life for our eternal souls. Take some time this week to thank him for his protecting love, and especially for his gift of salvation. Next week we will talk together about the hope that comes when we realize God's far-reaching plan.

NOTES ON JOHN 10:11–18

Summary: The "good shepherd" passage of John's gospel comes at the end of a short discourse in which Jesus uses the metaphor of the sheep and the shepherd to teach several things. Throughout, he emphasizes that the sheep who belong to him will recognize his voice when he calls them. Beginning in verse 11, Jesus draws a picture contrasting the behavior of the hired hand and the true shepherd. The hired hand cares more for his own skin than he does for the welfare of the sheep, because they are not his. But the good shepherd not only cares for the sheep, he loves them and is willing even to lay down his life for them. He compares the relationship between the sheep and the shepherd to his own relationship with the Father. He also stressed the fact that his death would be voluntary, and that he would rise again.

10:11 I am the good shepherd. In contrast to the hired hand who runs away at danger, the true shepherd cares for the flock at his own risk (1 Sam. 17:34–35). The image of the ruler as a shepherd was a very common one in Israel (Ps. 23; Ezek. 34).

10:14 I know My own sheep. While verse 11 highlighted the quality of sacrifice in the good shepherd, this verse highlights his personal awareness of the sheep. "To know" is equivalent with "to love" (v. 15).

10:16 I have other sheep that are not of this fold. Since this gospel has consistently stressed that Jesus' mission was not just for Jews but for all the world, it is likely that this is the meaning here also. **one flock, one shepherd.** The Christian community is not to be marred by divisions, but is to model unity across racial and ethnic lines as all respond to the voice of the one shepherd (John 11:52; Eph. 2:11–22).

10:18 I have the right to lay it down. Our security comes from the fact that we serve a powerful God. Jesus did not lose his life because it was taken from him by force. Jesus' death was not that of a martyr dying when things got out of control. To die and rise again was his Father's will for him. We can be reassured by the fact that God is still in control.

[1]Darlene Deibler Rose, *Evidence Not Seen* (San Fransisco, CA: Harper & Row Publishers, 1988), pp. 50-51.

Session 4
HOPE FOR THE JOURNEY
Scripture John 20:1–18

 ## LAST WEEK

In the session last week, we talked about the care and protection afforded us by God—sometimes physical protection from danger, as in the Life Story we read, but more importantly the protection we have from eternal death because of his voluntary sacrifice of his life. This week, we will catch a glimpse of the pattern of God's plan and see the hope that comes in the worst situations when we realize the very thing that seems irretrievably bad to us is being used by God for his perfect plan.

 ### Ice-Breaker : 15 min.
CONNECT WITH YOUR GROUP

Leader
Choose one, two or all three of the Ice-Breaker questions. Welcome and introduce new group members.

Hope was the one bright thing in Pandora's box of troubles. Take turns sharing with one another your own experiences with hope in darkness.

1   If you were going to describe your attitude toward hope in terms of light, what terms would you use?
    ○ A halogen floodlight: I'm a real optimist.
    ○ A trick birthday candle: the light is small, but it won't go out.
    ○ A reading lamp: it helps a lot, but the corners are still dark.
    ○ A moonless night: I can't see a thing.
    ○ Other _____.

2.   What was your biggest trial when you were a teenager? Did you have any hope that things would change?

3.   Do you think you are more or less hopeful now than you were when you were younger?

Study Time : 30 min.
READ + DISCUSS

LIFE STORY ILLUSTRATION

Hope in Isolation

We have already read a little about Corrie ten Boom and her experiences in prison during World War II. Once when she was ill, shortly before she and Betsie were sent to the concentration camp of Ravensbruck, she was thrown into an isolation cell. Even there, however, she found a message of hope from God. She tells of this in her book, *The Hiding Place*:

"In only one way was this new cell an improvement over the first one. It had a window. Seven iron bars ran across it, four bars up and down. It was high in the wall, much too high to look out of, but through those twenty-eight squares I could see the sky.

"All day I kept my eyes fixed on that bit of heaven. Sometimes clouds moved across the squares, white or pink or edged with gold, and when the wind was from the west I could hear the sea. Best of all, for nearly an hour each day, gradually lengthening as the spring sun rose higher, a shaft of checkered light streamed into the dark little room. As the weather turned warmer and I grew stronger I would stand up to catch the sunshine on my face and chest, moving along the wall with the moving light, climbing at last onto the cot to stand on tiptoe in the final rays.

"As my health returned, I was able to use my eyes longer. I had been sustaining myself from my Scriptures a verse at a time, now like a starving man I gulped entire Gospels at a reading, seeing whole the magnificent drama of salvation.

"And as I did, an incredible thought pricked the back of my neck. Was it possible that this—all of this that seemed so wasteful and so needless—this war, Scheveningen prison, this very cell, none of it was unforeseen or accidental? Could it be part of the pattern first revealed in the Gospels? Hadn't Jesus—and here my reading became intent indeed—hadn't Jesus been defeated as utterly and unarguably as our little group and our small plans had been?

"But … if the Gospels were truly the pattern of God's activity, then defeat was only the beginning. I would look around at the bare little cell and wonder what conceivable victory could come from a place like this."[1]

SCRIPTURE PASSAGE

Hoping is hard work. If hopes are dashed, one loses a lot of emotional energy. Many people in our society seem to have lost the energy to hope. They are struggling in the quicksand of despair, much like the disciples after Christ's crucifixion. The one upon whom they had placed so much hope was dead. Now what was left to live for? Only three days later they were transformed by joy as they found that their hopes were not lost in the grave with their dead teacher. Instead he was very much alive, and hope was alive too. Read John 20:1–18 and see how in God's plan what seemed like the ultimate defeat turned out to be the ultimate victory.

The Empty Tomb

20 On the first day of the week Mary Magdalene came to the tomb early, while it was still dark. She saw that the stone had been removed from the tomb. ²So she ran to Simon Peter and to the other disciple, whom Jesus loved, and said to them, "They have taken the Lord out of the tomb, and we don't know where they have put Him!"

³At that, Peter and the other disciple went out, heading for the tomb. ⁴The two were running together, but the other disciple outran Peter and got to the tomb first. ⁵Stooping down, he saw the linen cloths lying there, yet he did not go in. ⁶Then, following him, Simon Peter came also. He entered the tomb and saw the linen cloths lying there. ⁷The wrapping that had been on His head was not lying with the linen cloths but folded up in a separate place by itself. ⁸The other disciple, who had reached the tomb first, then entered the tomb, saw, and believed. ⁹For they still did not understand the Scripture that He must rise from the dead. ¹⁰Then the disciples went home again.

¹¹But Mary stood outside facing the tomb, crying. As she was crying, she stooped to look into the tomb. ¹²She saw two angels in white sitting there, one at the head and one at the feet, where Jesus' body had been lying. ¹³They said to her, "Woman, why are you crying?"

"Because they've taken away my Lord," she told them, "and I don't know where they've put Him." ¹⁴Having said this, she turned around and saw Jesus standing there, though she did not know it was Jesus.

¹⁵"Woman," Jesus said to her, "why are you crying? Who is it you are looking for?"

Supposing He was the gardener, she replied, "Sir, if you've removed Him, tell me where you've put Him, and I will take Him away."

¹⁶"Mary!" Jesus said.

Turning around, she said to Him in Hebrew, "Rabbouni!"—which means "Teacher."

¹⁷"Don't cling to Me," Jesus told her, "for I have not yet ascended to the Father. But go to My brothers and tell them that I am ascending to My Father and your Father—to My God and your God."

¹⁸Mary Magdalene went and announced to the disciples, "I have seen the Lord!" And she told them what He had said to her.

John 20:1–18

QUESTIONS FOR INTERACTION

Leader

Refer to the Summary and Study Notes at the conclusion of this session as needed. If 30 minutes is not enough time to answer all of the questions in this section, conclude the Bible Study by answering question 7.

1. Put yourself in the place of Mary. What is your emotional state two days after the Crucifixion? Why do you visit the tomb so early? Realizing that the body is gone, how do you react?

2. Do you think you would have responded more like Mary or like the disciples? Why?

3. Why do you think the "other disciple" did not go in, even though he ran hard to reach the tomb first?
   ○ He was afraid of tomb robbers.
   ○ He was queasy about maybe seeing a dead body.
   ○ He was afraid to hope.
   ○ He was looking for Jesus outside.
   ○ At the last minute he didn't want to see it alone.
   ○ Other_____.

4. Why do you think Mary Magdalene was so slow to recognize who Jesus was? What made her finally realize who he was?

5. When it comes to looking for hope in your own life, where are you right now in terms of this story?
   ○ Standing "outside the tomb" afraid to look.
   ○ Weeping for what I have lost and overlooking the presence of Christ.
   ○ Seeing the "empty tomb," but tending to interpret it as something bad.
   ○ Seeing the evidence of hope and believing.

6. Corrie ten Boom says that according to the pattern in the Gospels, "defeat is only the beginning." Can you see this pattern that she is talking about? Explain. In what ways have you seen defeat turn into victory in your own life?

7. In what way does the knowledge of Christ's resurrection affect your life right now?

GOING DEEPER:
If your group has time and/or wants a challenge, go on to this question.

8. What is your proof that Jesus rose from the dead?

Caring Time : 15 min.
APPLY THE LESSON AND PRAY FOR ONE ANOTHER

Leader

Be sure to save at least 15 minutes for this important time. After sharing responses to all three questions and asking for prayer requests, close in a time of group prayer.

Use this special time to bring each other hope and encouragement by sharing prayer requests and special concerns. Begin by sharing responses to the following questions, and don't forget to pray for someone to fill the empty chair.

1. Where is your "hope level" right now? How can this group pray for your needs?

2. How could you bring hope to someone in a difficult situation this week?

3. Do you have any special requests or praises this group can bring before the Lord?

NEXT WEEK

Today we read the exciting and hope-giving story of the resurrection of Jesus and looked at the way God works things that seem bad into a good situation that surpasses imagination. The true story of Corrie ten Boom's realization that her imprisonment was all part of God's good plan reinforces the idea that God is in control of every situation, and is more than able to turn defeat into sweet victory. It is this knowledge that gives believers a hope that would seem crazy to the rest of the world. During the coming week, consciously think about and thank God for the amazing hope that we have in the midst of the struggles of this life. Next week we will consider the importance of prayer as we seek strength for the journey of faith.

Summary: The week had begun with Jesus' triumphal entry into Jerusalem, and it ended in the heart-wrenching despair of his crucifixion. Early in the morning on the first day of the week, Mary went to the tomb to finish preparing the body and found him gone. Never thinking that he might be alive, she rushed back to the others distraught with the news that he had been stolen. Peter and another disciple ran to look, and finding what she said was true, turned around and went home. But Mary stayed and wept in despair. Even when the two angels and Jesus spoke to her, her only thought was to recover his body. And then Jesus called her name. One can only imagine Mary's intense joy and the joy of the disciples when they knew he was indeed risen.

20:1 the first day of the week. This was Sunday. **Mary Magdalene.** Mary is mentioned in all four gospel accounts of the Resurrection. Luke 8:2 says that she was one of several women who traveled with the disciples. Although the story is not told, Jesus cast seven demons out of her at some point. **stone.** This account of the burial of Jesus does not mention that it was sealed with a large stone, but see Matthew 27:60 and Mark 15:46.

20:3 the other disciple. This is still the "beloved disciple" mentioned in verse 2.

20:5-7 the linen cloths. Grave robbers, in search of treasures entombed with the corpse, would either have taken the body still wrapped up, or scattered the strips as they tore them off. The fact that the clothes were neatly laid by was one of the evidences that led the "other disciple" to faith (v. 8).

20:9 they still did not understand the Scripture. The Old Testament Scripture referred to is not certain. Isaiah 53:10-12 and Psalm 16:9-11 may be in view. These passages were used later on as evidence to show that the death and resurrection of the Messiah was foretold (Acts 2:25-28; 8:32-33), but that understanding came after further teaching from Jesus (Luke 24:45-47).

20:12 two angels in white. The gospels differ on whether there was one "man" (Mark), or an angel (Matthew), or two "men" (Luke) present. They also differ on how many women saw the personage. This author's point is to present the story of Mary as that of a typical disciple who came to realize the truth of the Resurrection.

20:13 Woman. Although in our day this would seem to be an impersonal, even rude, form of address, its usage in verse 15 and in 2:4 indicates that it was not necessarily that way in this culture.

20:14 she did not know it was Jesus. Later on, there is another scene when Jesus was not recognized at first (21:4; Luke 24:15-16). Paul speaks of the resurrected body as having a different type of splendor than the normal body (1 Cor. 15:40-42). Whether she was blinded by her intense grief or there was some type of transformation in

Jesus' appearance that caused Mary's lack of recognition is not known.

20:15 gardener. The tomb was located in a garden owned by Joseph (19:41). It would not be unlikely that as an aristocratic member of the Sanhedrin he would employ a gardener to care for his property.

20:16 "Mary." Jesus had said that the Good Shepherd "calls his own sheep by name" and that they "will listen to my voice" (10:3,16). When Jesus speaks Mary's name, she immediately recognizes who it is that speaks to her. **Rabbouni.** Literally, "my teacher." This is not only a title of respect for Jesus, but one that shows Mary's submission and love for him.

20:17 Don't cling to Me. We need not think Jesus refused to allow her to touch him at all, but that, after Mary had expressed the joy and relief she would feel at seeing him, he simply told her that all was not finished yet. Just as he had told the other disciples (14:15–20), he is reminding her that she will "hold on" to him in a far more personal way as soon as he returns to the Father; then he will come to her in the person of the Counselor, or Holy Spirit. **ascended to the Father.** The goal of being reunited with his Father in glory has dominated Jesus' teaching (13:36; 14:28; 16:10; 17:5,13). This announcement to Mary asserts that what he has long anticipated is now to occur. **go to My brothers.** Although the disciples have been called "servants" (13:16) and "friends" (15:15), this is the first time they have been called by this familial term (Heb. 2:10–18). **My Father and your Father / My God and your God.** Ruth 1:16 uses a similar formula to indicate Ruth's desire to establish the closest type of kinship possible with her mother-in-law Naomi. By using this phrase, Jesus is reinforcing what he said about the unity between he, the believer, and the Father (14:15–23; 16:27). By virtue of his sacrificial death on their behalf, they now have the same access to the Father that he has.

20:18 I have seen the Lord! The riddle of John 16:16 has come to pass for Mary. The title "Lord" carries the full weight of its divine meaning (11:27). The disciples' reaction to her is not given here, but Luke 24:11 says they did not believe this testimony.

[1]Corrie ten Boom, *The Hiding Place* (Minneapolis, MN: World Wide Publications, 1971), p. 157.

Session 5

STRENGTH FOR THE JOURNEY

Scripture Luke 11:1–13

 ## LAST WEEK

In last week's lesson, we were encouraged as we saw the great hope that comes from realizing God's plan. The apparent defeat of the Cross was the beginning of the great victory over sin and death. Corrie ten Boom realized that, even though she had a hard time imagining what good could come out of it, her imprisonment would be used by God for his glory. What a difference it makes to know that God is in control, and nothing is wasted. Today we will look at another source of encouragement and strength that God has provided. We will learn what Jesus has to say about prayer as he teaches his disciples.

 ## Ice Breaker : 15 min.
CONNECT WITH YOUR GROUP

Leader

Choose one or two of the Ice-Breaker questions. If you have a new group member you may want to do all three. Remember to stick closely to the three-part agenda and the time allowed for each segment.

Often one of the best ways to find encouragement is to spend some time with a good friend, just talking and enjoying one another's company. Fellowship is an important part of a healthy life. Take some time now to enjoy one another as you answer the following questions.

1. When you want to relax, what kind of atmosphere do you tend to choose?
   ○ A party with friends where I can just be myself and have fun.
   ○ A quiet room with a book and a fireplace and a "Do Not Disturb" sign.
   ○ A huge mall and a friend who loves to shop as much as I do.
   ○ An evening at home with my family and no outside activities.
   ○ A hike in the great outdoors.
   ○ Other_____.

2. When you were a child or teen, were you more likely to be shy and quiet or the outgoing type with a hundred friends? Are you the same now or have you changed?

3. Do you ever talk to yourself? What do you talk about?

 | **Study Time: 30 min.**
READ ÷ DISCUSS

LIFE STORY ILLUSTRATION

Fatima's Prayer

Patricia St. John spent many years as a missionary in Morocco, first as a nurse in a large hospital in Tangier and later in her own house in a small mountain town. She experienced herself the very real strength and direction that comes through prayer, and she also had the privilege of seeing God work in the lives of others in the same way. In her autobiography, *An Ordinary Woman's Extraordinary Faith*, she tells the story of one of the women who experienced the power of prayer. Fatima was a young woman with one child and a husband who was a drug addict. She came every day to help out in the dispensary, initially because they knew she needed the help, but soon because she became indispensable to the work. She listened, uncomprehending at first, to their daily Bible reading and prayer, and some of the stories interested her very much—particularly the loaves and fishes.

"Then one morning she arrived sobbing bitterly and furiously angry. She had gone home the night before to find an empty house. Her husband had gone to another woman and taken everything they possessed—blankets, cooking pot, everything—and she had no appeal apart from bribes and influential friends, and of those she had none. She sat for a long time, cursing him, calling him names, and weeping. She never wished to see him again, she sobbed.

" 'Then why are you so angry he's gone?' I asked.

" 'I'm not crying for my husband,' she replied angrily, 'I'm crying for my blankets.'

"We shared what we could, and Marguerite stitched some curtains. The essentials of life were very cheap, and for a time she was, perhaps, happier without the man. But one day she arrived almost mad with grief, and this time there was no comforting her. Her husband had taken [her daughter] Tamoo as a little servant, as his new wife was pregnant, and once again there seemed to be no appeal. It was not etiquette to visit the house of your ex-husband, and the only time she ever saw the child was at the well. These were miserable meetings, for Tamoo looked thin and dirty, with sores on her head and arms. She cried to come home to her mother.

"And then the possibility of prayer dawned on Fatima, and she suggested that we ask God to bring her daughter back. To my weak faith it seemed an unlikely event. The new baby was due, and little slaves of seven are extremely useful, but we started to pray daily. I cannot remember for how long we prayed, but it was mid-winter before the answer was given.

"Winter in that town was a dreary season. ... On [one] cold night of wind and rain I was glad to get into bed and go to sleep.

"But I was woken by a loud knocking and I ran to the window. A woman stood at the door, bowed with some heavy weight under her haik, and beckoning franticaly. I went down and opened the door. Fatima almost fell through it. She flung off her haik, revealing Tamoo gasping and coughing on her back.

"There was no doubt that the child had pneumonia. So we propped her up with pillows and tucked her into bed. We gave her antibiotics and cough mixture and a hot drink and she fell into a restless sleep. And then Fatima told her story. Neighbors had told her that her daughter was ill, and she was lying awake grieving for her with the rain dripping through the roof, when she said she was suddenly conscious of a presence in the room. She could not tell how, but somehow she knew it was Jesus, and he said to her, "Go and fetch your daughter." Fatima explained that this was impossible. It was raining hard, she could not go out alone in the dark—and it was against all convention to visit her ex-husband. But the presence and the voice persisted, "Go and fetch your daughter." So she got up and wrapped her haik around her and went out into the night.

"Arriving at the door, she stood for a long time, listening. She could hear a child crying, but no one took any notice. In the end she tried the metal ring and to her amazement the door was unlocked, and she stole inside. It took another long time to persuade herself that the house was empty except for her crying child, but at last she dared approach the bed and lifted Tamoo on to her back. No one stopped her, for there was no one there. She hurried through the dark, silent streets to our house, like Peter freed from prison, wondering if it was all a dream.

"Her father never asked for Tamoo again, and the incident was quite easily explained. He had gone away for a night on business and his wife, who was very young and foolish, saw that Tamoo was seriously ill. *If I am here when she dies*, thought the poor creature, *my husband will say that I am responsible. It would be better not to be here.* So she took her baby and herself off to her mother's house for the night. But what no one could explain was the presence of Jesus caring for that child and restoring her to her mother, and Fatima did not try to explain. She accepted what had happened in a matter-of-fact way, and it was probably at that point that she decided to become a Christian. After all, if he could feed five thousand with five loaves and two fishes, nothing could surprise her any more."[1]

SCRIPTURE PASSAGE

God really does answer prayers and prayer is an important part of the walk of faith, but sometimes we have a hard time knowing how to pray. Read Luke 11:1–13 and listen to Jesus' teaching on prayer.

The Lord's Prayer

11 He was praying in a certain place, and when He finished, one of His disciples said to Him, "Lord, teach us to pray, just as John also taught his disciples."

²He said to them, "Whenever you pray, say:

Father, Your name be honored as holy.
Your kingdom come.
³   Give us each day our daily bread.
⁴   And forgive us our sins,
for we ourselves also forgive everyone in debt to us.
And do not bring us into temptation."

⁵He also said to them: "Suppose one of you has a friend and goes to him at midnight and says to him, 'Friend, lend me three loaves of bread, ⁶because a friend of mine on a journey has come to me, and I don't have anything to offer him.' ⁷Then he will answer from inside and say, 'Don't bother me! The door is already locked, and my children and I have gone to bed. I can't get up to give you anything.' ⁸I tell you, even though he won't get up and give him anything because he is his friend, yet because of his persistence, he will get up and give him as much as he needs.

⁹"So I say to you, keep asking, and it will be given to you. Keep searching, and you will find. Keep knocking, and the door will be opened to you. ¹⁰For everyone who asks receives, and the one who searches finds, and to the one who knocks, the door will be opened. ¹¹What father among you, if his son asks for a fish, will, instead of a fish, give him a snake? ¹²Or if he asks for an egg, will give him a scorpion? ¹³If you then, who are evil, know how to give good gifts to your children, how much more will the heavenly Father give the Holy Spirit to those who ask Him?"

Luke 11:1–13

 QUESTIONS FOR INTERACTION

Leader

Refer to the Summary and Study Notes at the conclusion of this session as needed. If 30 minutes is not enough time to answer all of the questions in this section, conclude the Bible Study by answering questions 6 and 7.

1. What do you do to prepare for prayer?
   ○ Read a psalm.
   ○ Sing.
   ○ Use a devotional guide.
   ○ Other_____.

2. Do you think your faith is more like Fatima's (praying for the impossible) or would you tend to respond more like Patricia (not thinking that it would really happen)?

3. What "good gifts" are you wanting from God right now?

4. What are the basic elements of the Lord's prayer in this passage? Do you see this as a prayer to be memorized and repeated as is, or as a pattern for extemporaneous prayer? Why?

5. What does the parable in verses 5–8 teach about prayer?

6. What concerns occupy most of your time in prayer?
   ○ Praise.
   ○ Confession.
   ○ Petition.
   ○ Complaining.
   ○ Other_____.

   In what areas do you need to grow?

7. What do you see as the central point of this passage, in one sentence?

 GOING DEEPER:
If your group has time and/or wants a challenge, go on to this question.

---

8. How can you reconcile verses 9 and 10 with the times when your prayers seem to go unanswered? Have you ever had a "no" answer to a request for what seemed like a "good gift"? Why do you think he said no?

Caring Time : 15 min.
APPLY THE LESSON AND PRAY FOR ONE ANOTHER

Leader
Continue to encourage group members to invite new people to the group. Remind everyone that this group is for learning and sharing, but also for reaching out to others. Close the group prayer by thanking God for each member and for this time together.

Before we close this session, we have the opportunity to practice what we studied today. Take turns sharing the answers to the following questions, and then close with prayer.

1. When you pray, how confident do you feel that God will hear you?
   - ○ I think I need a megaphone.
   - ○ He knows what I need before I even say it.
   - ○ I can talk to him like my best friend.
   - ○ I feel as if I'm talking to a brick wall.
   - ○ Other_____.

2. How can we in this group help one another to grow in prayer as we talked about in question 6?

3. Do you have any other requests you would like to share with the group?

NEXT WEEK

Today we discussed the subject of prayer, specifically looking at the teaching of Jesus when his disciples asked how to pray. We considered how we can grow in our prayer lives, and we were encouraged as we read a true story of how God answered the prayer of a woman in a very difficult circumstance. During the coming week, commit to spending a little time each day in prayer. Next week we will find further strength for the journey as we study some of God's special promises to us.

Summary: Jesus' disciples saw him praying, and asked to be taught how. Jesus responded with a short model prayer, and a parable about persistence in prayer. He assured the disciples that those who seek God will not seek in vain, and that God is prepared to bestow good gifts upon his children; specifically the gift of the Holy Spirit.

11:1 teach us to pray. Various Jewish groups (including John's disciples) had their own distinctive prayers. The issue of whether Jesus was here seeking to teach a specific rote prayer or simply some principles of what should be included in prayer is much debated. The prayer (and its counterpart in Matthew 6:9–13) does contain the elements of praise ("Your name be honored as holy"), submission ("Your kingdom come"), petition for physical need ("Give us each day our daily bread"), and petition for spiritual need ("forgive us our sins ... do not bring us not into temptation").

11:2 Father. While even the orthodox Jews of the day called God "our Father," this simple, personal form of address was new. Jesus normally used the term *Abba*, a term more akin to "Dad" than "Father," which was being much more familiar with God than other rabbis thought appropriate. He is teaching the disciples to approach God personally. (See also Romans 8:15 and Galatians 4:6 where Paul indicates that followers of Christ felt free to use this familiar term because of their association with Christ.) **Your name be honored as holy.** The first petition is that the name of God (i.e., his character and nature) be honored by all. **Your kingdom come.** The prayer is that God will quickly establish the reign of his kingdom throughout the world. We are called to make the coming of the kingdom of God our top priority in Matthew 6:33: "But seek first the kingdom of God and His righteousness, and all these things will be provided for you." While the kingdom is in some sense already present, it will only come in its fullness when Christ returns.

11:3 our daily bread. This request resonates with the remembrance of God's provision of manna for the Israelites in the wilderness (Ex. 16:18).

11:4 for we ourselves also forgive. This is not an appeal for forgiveness as a reward for our forgiving others, but rather a reminder that to receive God's forgiveness necessarily implies a willingness to extend that to others. Jesus told the Parable of the Unmerciful Servant (Matt. 18:21–35) to make exactly this point. **do not bring us into temptation.** The request is that the person will not have to face a trial so difficult that she will fall into sin. The apostle Paul underlined that God indeed would respond to this petition faithfully: "No temptation has overtaken you except what is common to humanity. God is faithful and He will not allow you to be tempted beyond what you are able, but with the temptation He will also provide a way of escape, so that you are able to bear it" (1 Cor. 10:13).

11:5–6 Hospitality was a value held in high regard in the ancient Middle East, perhaps because so many people groups were nomadic. Lot went to great lengths to provide safety and hospitality to the angels (whom he thought were just men) who visited Sodom; and the author of Hebrews, with stories like that in mind, urged Christians to continue to be hospitable to traveling strangers (Heb. 13:2). Since hospitality was such an important duty, it would be urgent that the host in this story provide some food for his surprise visitor.

11:8 his persistence. Literally, "shamelessness." The interpretation of the parable can go two ways depending on which man is meant by this phrase. If it is the boldness of the man approaching his friend so late, then the parable is meant to encourage the disciples to be persistent in prayer, a lesson more clearly taught in 18:1–8. If, however, the householder is in view, then the parable means that since even a *man* would go to such lengths so as not to be known as one who would refuse a friend in need, certainly *God* will not fail to respond to the needs of those who pray to him. None of this is to say that God gives us everything we ask for. The promise is that God will respond to meet the need. But God always knows how to meet our needs better than we do.

11:9 keep asking / searching / knocking. Each of these verbs is a present imperative, which therefore means "keep on asking," keep on searching," and "keep on knocking." This emphasizes the fact that prayer is a continuous, ongoing process. Prayer is rooted in the assurance that the householder (God) will arise and meet the need of his friend. By this teaching, Jesus reinforces the Old Testament promises that God will be found by those who seek him in repentance and faith (Deut. 4:29; Isa. 55:6–7; 65:1; Jer. 29:12). It should be warned, however, that parables are not intended to be exact parallels to the life situation to which they speak. God is not, in fact, surly and hesitant to respond to our needs. Nor does he engage in sleep, from which we have to wake him to get his attention!

11:11–12 Once again Jesus uses an analogy to make his point. The way a father treats his child can be a model for how God treats his children. **fish / egg.** These were common foods for people in Galilee. **snake / scorpion.** These were animals that Jews were forbidden to eat (Lev. 11:12,42). The snake may be an eel-like fish that likewise was forbidden to the Jews. The scorpion, at least, could be poisonous.

11:13 who are evil. This is a strong statement. The word "evil" is used elsewhere to characterize Satan (Matt. 6:13). The point of the analogy is that since not even a sinful human father would give such a repulsive, dangerous food to his own son, how much less will the perfect heavenly Father fail to give what his children most need? **the Holy Spirit.** In the parallel account, Matthew 7:11 says "good gifts" with an obviously spiritual intent in mind. Luke's version reflects the fact that the fullness of God's gift to his people is found in the presence of his Spirit with his people.

Patricia St. John, *An Ordinary Woman's Extraordinary Faith* (Wheaton, IL: Harold Shaw Publishers, 1993), pp.112-115.

Session 6
PROMISES FOR THE JOURNEY
Scripture Luke 12:22-34

LAST WEEK

In last week's session, we studied Jesus' teaching on prayer and talked together about how prayer affects our lives, and how important it is. This week we will find strength in the unbreakable promises of God as we learn to put our trust in them. God is looking after each of us, caring for our eternal destiny.

Ice-Breaker : 15 min.
CONNECT WITH YOUR GROUP

Leader
Introduce and welcome new group members. If there are no new members, choose two or three of the Ice-Breaker questions to get started.

Dealing with the cares of our daily life sometimes seems to take up more than its fair share of time. Take turns now sharing your experiences about keeping up with your life.

1. Do you tend to "have your ducks in a row" in your daily life, or do you suffer from "nonlinear waterfowl disorder"?

2. When you were a child, were you more likely to worry about things or to assume that the adults had it all under control?

3. When you go on a trip, how do you get ready?
   ○ I make reservations early and pack several days before I need to leave.
   ○ I forget to pack until an hour before departure.
   ○ I never plan a trip at all—just hop in the car and go when the mood strikes.
   ○ I always plan my itinerary down to the minute, and keep to my schedule.
   ○ I like to plan ahead but still leave room to be spontaneous.
   ○ Other_____.

Study Time: 30 min.
READ ÷ DISCUSS

Leader
Ahead of time, ask two members of the group to read aloud the Life Story and the Scripture passage. Then discuss the Questions for Interaction, dividing into subgroups of three to six.

LIFE STORY ILLUSTRATION

The Prison Riot

Gladys Aylward spent many years in China as a missionary. Most of her time there was spent in the remote mountain provinces where she worked for the Chinese government as the official foot inspector, supervising the unbinding of little girls feet and taking the opportunity to preach the Gospel in every village she visited. Gladys' biography, *The Small Woman,* tells of one instance where she was forced to put the promises of God to the test. She was called to the local men's prison. Not understanding why she was singled out, she responded with the messenger sent to bring her.

"They hurried up the road and in through the East Gate. A few yards inside the gate the blank outside wall of the prison flanked the main street. From the other side came an unholy noise: screams, shouts, yells, the most horrible sounds. ... The governor of the prison, small, pale-faced, his mouth set into a worried line, met her at the entrance. Behind were grouped half a dozen of his staff.

"'We are glad you have come,' he said quickly. 'There is a riot in the prison; the convicts are killing each other.'...

" 'I'm sorry to hear that,' said Gladys. 'But what do you expect me to do about it? I don't even know why you asked me to come. ...'

"The governor took a step forward. 'You must go in and stop the fighting!'

" 'I must go in! Are you mad? If I went in they'd kill me!'

"The governor's eyes were fixed on her with hypnotic urgency. 'But how can they kill you? You have been telling everybody that you have come here because you have the living God inside you. ...'

"Gladys felt a small, cold shiver down her back. When she swallowed, her throat seemed to have a gritty texture.

" 'The—living God?' she stammered.

" 'You preach it everywhere, in the streets and villages. If you preach the truth— if your God protects you from harm—then you can stop this riot.' She stared at him. ... A little cell in her mind kept blinking on and off with an urgent semaphore message: 'It's true! You have been preaching that your Christian God protects you from harm. Fail now and you are finished in Yangcheng. Abandon your faith now and you abandon it forever!" It was a desperate challenge. ... But how could she go into the prison with those men—murderers, thieves, bandits—rioting and killing each other inside those walls! By the sounds, louder now, a small human hell had broken loose. How could she? 'I must try,' she said to herself. 'I must try. Oh, God, give me strength.'...

" 'All right,' she said. 'Open the door. I'll go in to them.' ... Literally she was pushed inside. It was dark. The door closed behind her. ... She was locked in the prison with a horde of raving criminals who by their din sounded as if they had all gone insane. ... With faltering footsteps, she walked [to the courtyard] and came to an abrupt standstill, rooted in horror. ... Within its confines a writhing fiendish battle was going on. Several bodies were stretched out on the flagstones. ... There was blood everywhere. ... The main group of men ... [was] watching one convict who brandished a large, bloodstained chopper. As she stared, he suddenly rushed at them and they scattered wildly to every part of the square. ... No one took any notice whatsoever of Gladys. For fully half a minute she stood motionless with no idea what to do. The man rushed again; the group parted; he singled one man out and chased him. The man ran toward Gladys, then ducked away. The madman with the axe halted only a few feet from her. Without any plan, hardly realizing what she was doing, she instinctively took two angry steps toward him.

" 'Give me that chopper,' she said furiously. 'Give it to me at once!'

"The man looked at her. For three long seconds the wild, dark pupils, staring from bloodshot eyes, glared at her. He took two paces forward. Then suddenly, meekly, he held out the axe."[1]

SCRIPTURE PASSAGE

Gladys had to trust God to preserve her life as she walked into the prison. Even though we don't always think of it this way, we need to trust God to preserve our lives every day. Read Luke 12:22–34 and thank God for his promises to care for us.

Don't Worry

[22]Then He said to His disciples: "Therefore I tell you, don't worry about your life, what you will eat; or about the body, what you will wear. [23]For life is more than food and the body more than clothing. [24]Consider the ravens: they don't sow or reap; they don't have a storeroom or a barn; yet God feeds them. Aren't you worth much more than the birds? [25]Can any of you add a cubit to his height by worrying? [26]If then you're not able to do even a little thing, why worry about the rest?

[27]"Consider how the wildflowers grow: they don't labor or spin thread. Yet I tell you, not even Solomon in all his splendor was adorned like one of these! [28]If that's how God clothes the grass, which is in the field today and is thrown into the furnace tomorrow, how much more will He do for you—you of little faith? [29]Don't keep striving for what you should eat and what you should drink, and do not be anxious. [30]For the Gentile world eagerly seeks all these things, and your Father knows that you need them.

[31]"But seek His kingdom, and these things will be provided for you. [32]Don't be afraid, little flock, because your Father delights to give you the kingdom. [33]Sell your possessions and give to the poor. Make money-bags for yourselves that won't grow old, an inexhaustible treasure in heaven, where no thief comes near and no moth destroys. [34]For where your treasure is, there your heart will be also.

Luke 12:22-34

QUESTIONS FOR INTERACTION

Leader

Refer to the Summary and Study Notes at the end of this session as needed. If 30 minutes is not enough time to answer all of the questions in this section, conclude the Bible Study by answering question 8.

1. What is the worry level in your life right now?
   - ○ No sweat, everything is under control.
   - ○ On the verge of panic.
   - ○ I have a few worries but nothing serious.
   - ○ I have a lot to worry about, but I'm working on turning it over to the Lord.
   - ○ Other_____.

2. What are your biggest "worry triggers"? Do you tend to worry about the future, or about things in your present life?

3. Have you ever had to worry about your daily needs for food, clothing and shelter? How did you handle it?

4. In your own life, do you think you would have a harder time trusting God in a really dangerous situation like Gladys, or would actually relying on Him to provide daily food seem like a bigger step of faith?

5. What is the lesson Jesus wants his disciples to learn in this passage? How does not worrying work out practically in your life? What about working for your living?

6. What does Jesus mean when he talks about making "money-bags that won't grow old," and a "treasure in heaven"? What do you usually consider to be your greatest treasures?

7. Who is someone you admire because they live in the tension of a pagan world (v. 30) with kingdom values (v. 31)? What can you do to "seek His kingdom"?

8. When you find yourself consumed with worry and anxiety, what do you do? How can you actually turn this over to the Lord and not worry? What do you think it would take for you to realize that "your Father delights to give you the kingdom"?

GOING DEEPER:

If your group has time and/or wants a challenge, go on to this question.

9. What is the kernel of Jesus' teaching in verse 33? How far do you think you can take the injunction to sell all your belongings and give to the poor?

Caring Time : 15 min.

APPLY THE LESSON AND PRAY FOR ONE ANOTHER

Leader

Conclude the prayer time by asking God for guidance in determining the future mission and outreach of this group.

Anxiety and fear are crippling obstacles on the journey of faith. Take turns sharing the answers to the following questions before spending time supporting one another in prayer.

1. What specific worries and fears do you need to turn over to God? How can this group pray for you?

2. In what ways has this group been an encouragement to you?

3. How would you rate this past week?
   - ○ Dreadful.
   - ○ Dull.
   - ○ Nice and pleasant.
   - ○ Not the greatest.
   - ○ I was so busy I didn't notice what it was like.
   - ○ Just wonderful!

NEXT WEEK.

Today we focused on some of the wonderful promises of God. We discussed that we have no need to worry—in fact we have been commanded not to worry—because God will take care of us. This week, focus on turning your worries over to God, and tell him that you trust him for all of your concerns. Ask him what you can do to seek his kingdom and store up treasure in heaven. Next week we will see how God unexpectedly meets our needs with special blessings.

Summary: In the previous verses, Jesus told a story of a man who expended all of his energy in storing up for his future needs, only to die before he could use any of it. Jesus goes on to tell his disciples not to worry about what they would eat or wear. Just as God cares for the plants and animals he will care for us. Rather than seeking our own security we should seek the kingdom of God. It is not that we are not expected to work, but we do not need to carry the burden of worrying about our lives.

12:22 don't worry. Worry is rooted in the fear that ultimately I must take care of myself rather than trust God to do so. This prohibition does not mean that disciples need not do anything to feed and clothe themselves. What is commended is faith, not idleness.

12:23 Since all his possessions could not help the rich man at his death, why occupy oneself with them?

12:24 Consider the ravens. Birds, unable to either plant their own food or store it away, are an example of daily dependence upon God to meet one's needs.

12:25 a cubit to his height. Jesus is points out the futility of worrying about something we cannot possibly change.

12:27 wildflowers. In spite of the transitory nature of plants like field grass and flowers, which can do nothing to make their own beauty, God provides them with raiment that rivals that of Israel's most exalted king (2 Chron. 9:13–28).

12:28 you of little faith. Faith is reliance on the love, care and power of God. Faith is the opposite of anxiety.

12:29 Don't keep striving. Literally, "do not seek."

12:31 seek His kingdom. Having warned the disciples not to direct their attention toward the material benefits of this life, Jesus now encourages them to seek the spiritual blessings of God's kingdom.

12:33 moth. Although expensive clothing was a favorite form of wealth, it had the unfortunate drawback of being especially susceptible to insignificant creatures like moths. The treasure of heaven is unassailable (1 Peter 1:4).

12:34 A person's heart loyalty is shown by the type of treasure one accumulates. The treasure of one who seeks God's kingdom is found in the hands of the poor to whom he or she has generously given (v. 33).

¹Alan Burgess, *The Small Woman* (New York, NY: E. P. Dutton & Co., Inc., 1957), pp. 86-90.

Session 7

BLESSINGS FOR THE JOURNEY

Scripture **John 11:17–44**

 ## LAST WEEK

In last week's session, we explored the problem of worry versus trust in God's promises. We were encouraged by the knowledge that God is looking after us in our day-to-day lives as well as in our eternal destiny. This week we will see further examples of God's care for us as we read two different stories of sisters who experienced a special blessing in a very difficult situation.

 ## Ice-Breaker : 15 min.
CONNECT WITH YOUR GROUP

Leader
Choose one, two or all three Ice-Breaker questions, depending on your group's needs.

Some days seem to have more blessings than others. Take turns sharing some of the ups and downs you've encountered on your journey through life.

1. How would you describe the "road" that you are on at this point in your life?
   - ○ Rough and rocky.
   - ○ Steep and exhausting.
   - ○ Smooth and easy.
   - ○ All uphill.
   - ○ One big muddy pothole.
   - ○ Other_____.

2. At this point in your life, which is longer: your list of blessings or your "to do" list?

3. In the last week, what was your biggest blessing? What was your lowest point?

Leader

Select two members of the group ahead of time to read aloud the Life Story and the Scripture passage. Then discuss the Questions for Interaction, dividing into subgroups as necessary.

LIFE STORY ILLUSTRATION

The "Bottomless" Vitamin Bottle

Corrie ten Boom and her family sheltered Jews from the Nazi's in Holland during World War II. Eventually they were betrayed, and the whole family was sent off to prison. The others were scattered, but Corrie and her sister Betsie were sent to the same camp. Life in these camps was horrendous, but still God provided. In her autobiography, *The Hiding Place*, Corrie tells of a bottle of vitamins they had managed to bring with them and the special blessing God sent them through it.

"Another strange thing was happening. The Davitamon bottle was continuing to produce drops. It scarcely seemed possible, so small a bottle, so many doses a day. Now, in addition to Betsie, a dozen others on our pier were taking it.

"My instinct was always to hoard it—Betsie was growing so very weak! But others were ill as well. It was hard to say no to eyes that burned with fever, hands that shook with chill. I tried to save it for the very weakest—but even those soon numbered fifteen, twenty, twenty-five... .

"And still, every time I tilted the bottle, a drop appeared at the tip of the glass stopper. ...

"'There was a woman in the Bible,' Betsie said, 'whose oil jar was never empty.' She turned to it in the Book of Kings, the story of the poor widow of Zarephath who gave Elijah a room in her home: 'The jar of meal wasted not, neither did the cruse of oil fail, according to the word of Jehovah which he spoke by Elijah.'

"... It was one thing to believe that such things were possible thousands of years ago, another to have it happen now, to us, this very day. And yet it happened, this day, and the next, until an awed little group of spectators stood around watching the drops fall into the daily rations of bread.

"Many nights I lay awake in the shower of straw dust from the mattress above, trying to fathom the marvel of supply lavished upon us. 'Maybe,' I whispered to Betsie, 'only a molecule or two really gets through that little pinhole—and then in the air it expands!'

"I heard her soft laughter in the dark. 'Don't try to explain it Corrie, Just accept it as a surprise from a Father who loves you.'"[1]

SCRIPTURE PASSAGE

Jesus' own resurrection is not the only one spoken of in Scripture or even the New Testament. Here Jesus raises Lazaus from the dead, in a kind of foreshadowing of his own resurrection. Lazarus was the brother of Mary and Martha, two of Jesus' most faithful followers. Previous to this story, word had been sent to Jesus that Lazarus was ill, but Jesus delayed in returning and in the interim Lazarus died. Read John 11:17–44 and note how Jesus brings a very special blessing to a time of mourning.

Jesus Raises Lazarus

¹⁷*When Jesus arrived, He found that Lazarus had already been in the tomb four days. ¹⁸Bethany was near Jerusalem (about two miles away). ¹⁹Many of the Jews had come to Martha and Mary to comfort them about their brother. ²⁰As soon as Martha heard that Jesus was coming, she went to meet Him. But Mary remained seated in the house.*

²¹*Then Martha said to Jesus, "Lord, if You had been here, my brother wouldn't have died. ²²Yet even now I know that whatever You ask from God, God will give You."*

²³*"Your brother will rise again," Jesus told her.*

²⁴*Martha said, "I know that he will rise again in the resurrection at the last day."*

²⁵*Jesus said to her, "I am the resurrection and the life. The one who believes in Me, even if he dies, will live. ²⁶Everyone who lives and believes in Me will never die—ever. Do you believe this?"*

²⁷*"Yes, Lord," she told Him, "I believe You are the Messiah, the Son of God, who was to come into the world."*

²⁸*Having said this, she went back and called her sister Mary, saying in private, "The Teacher is here and is calling for you."*

²⁹*As soon as she heard this, she got up quickly and went to Him. ³⁰Jesus had not yet come into the village, but was still in the place where Martha had met Him. ³¹The Jews who were with her in the house consoling her saw that Mary got up quickly and went out. So they followed her, supposing that she was going to the tomb to cry there.*

³²*When Mary came to where Jesus was and saw Him, she fell at His feet and told Him, "Lord, if You had been here, my brother would not have died!"*

³³*When Jesus saw her crying, and the Jews who had come with her crying, He was angry in His spirit and deeply moved. ³⁴"Where have you put him?" He asked.*

"Lord," they told Him, "come and see."

³⁵*Jesus wept.*

³⁶*So the Jews said, "See how He loved him!" ³⁷But some of them said, "Couldn't He who opened the blind man's eyes also have kept this man from dying?"*

³⁸*Then Jesus, angry in Himself again, came to the tomb. It was a cave, and a stone was lying against it. ³⁹"Remove the stone," Jesus said.*

Martha, the dead man's sister, told Him, "Lord, he already stinks. It's been four days."

⁴⁰*Jesus said to her, "Didn't I tell you that if you believed you would see the glory of God?"*

⁴¹*So they removed the stone. Then Jesus raised His eyes and said, "Father, I thank You that You heard Me. ⁴²I know that You always hear Me, but because of the crowd standing here I said this, so they may believe You sent Me." ⁴³After He said this, He shouted with a loud voice, "Lazarus, come out!" ⁴⁴The dead man came out bound hand and foot with linen strips and with his face wrapped in a cloth. Jesus said to them, "Loose him and let him go."*

John 11:17–44

QUESTIONS FOR INTERACTION

Leader

Refer to the Summary and Study Notes at the conclusion of this session as needed. If 30 minutes is not enough time to answer all of the questions in this section, conclude the Bible Study by answering question 7.

1. What blessings has God given to you this week? What has been the greatest blessing in your life?

2. Are you more likely to try and come up with a "scientific" explanation, or do you quickly recognize the hand of God in unusual circumstances in your life? How do you think your perceptions might change if you were to start looking back at your life trying to see where God has blessed you?

3. If you had been one of the sisters in the concentration camp, do you think you would have responded more like Betsie or like Corrie? What about Lazarus' sisters? Do you think you would have been able to look forward to the last day like Martha, or would you have been as distraught as Mary?

4. What is the relationship between sorrow or trouble and blessing? In what way might difficulty enhance a gift from God?

5. What is the significance of Jesus' statement to Martha that he is "the resurrection and the life" (vv. 25–26)? Since Martha said she believed this, why do you think she was shocked when Jesus asked them to roll away the stone?

6. How were Mary's and Martha's expectations of Jesus different? Which one do you think understood him better? Why do you think this?

7. Jesus loved Martha and Mary so much that he wept with them in their sorrow, even though he knew that he would restore their brother to them in just a few minutes. Betsie attributed their "bottomless vitamin bottle" to the same love. When have you felt this compassionate love of God in your life?

GOING DEEPER:

If your group has time and/or wants a challenge, go on to this question.

8. Why did Jesus raise Lazarus from the dead when he would just have to die again later? What would you say to the question in verse 37, which the others at the funeral asked?

Caring Time : 15 min.
APPLY THE LESSON AND PRAY FOR ONE ANOTHER

Leader
Following the Caring Time, discuss with your group how they would like to celebrate the last session next week. Also, discuss the possibility of splitting into two groups continuing together with the possibility of another study.

One of the ways God blesses us is with caring friends to support us along the way. Take turns sharing the answers to the following questions, and then close in a time of group prayer.

1. What special blessing would you like to thank God for right now?

2. If you were going to use the Lazarus' story to describe your spiritual life right now, where would you be?
   ○ Sick in bed.
   ○ In the tomb.
   ○ Alive, but tangled up in the grave clothes.
   ○ Alive and free.

3. Do you have some sorrow in your life where you need to know that Jesus has not abandoned you, as Mary felt? How can this group pray for you?

NEXT WEEK

Today we gave special thought to recognizing the blessings that God has brought into our lives. Our blessing lists are actually longer than we think, it is just that sometimes we forget to notice and appreciate those blessings. This week, set aside some time to thank God for the love that he shows you, and be on the lookout for his blessings in your life. Next week we will conclude this study with one more lesson of encouragement as we look for joy in the journey of faith.

NOTES ON JOHN 11:17–44

Summary: Jesus had spent a great deal of time in the home of Martha and Mary and their brother. No one could understand why he did not rush to their side when he heard that Lazarus was ill, but he delayed long enough that when he arrived Lazarus was already dead. Martha was grieved deeply at the loss of her brother, but she displayed a touching trust in Jesus. She believed that God would give him whatever he asked. Even so, when Jesus promised her that her brother would rise, she assumed that he only meant on the last day. Jesus then explained to her the truth in one of the most spine-tingling verses of Scripture: "I am the resurrection and the life … The one who believes in Me, even if he dies, will live. …" Martha's response shows that she understood part of the tremendous impact of his words. Only of the Messiah could such an incredible statement be true. This passage also pictures the tremendous love and compassion of Jesus. Even though he knew that he would restore their brother in just a few minutes, he wept with them in their deep grief. In the dramatic scene where Jesus calls Lazarus out, he makes sure that everyone present realizes where his power comes from. The whole situation was allowed to happen so that people could know who sent him and glorify God. Jesus' last comment is almost comical after such an incredible miracle—he just casually suggests that one of the astonished onlookers unwrap poor Lazarus.

11:21 if You had been here, my brother wouldn't have died. Since Lazarus had died probably even before Jesus received the message, and since Martha also adds a statement of trust in Christ's power to do something won-derful "even now" (v. 22) this is not a rebuke but an expression of regret. It implies faith that if Jesus had been on the scene before his death, Lazarus could have been saved.

11:22 Yet even now I know. Given

her confusion in verse 39, this may not be an expectation that Jesus could do a miracle even now. However, it is an expression of a faith that Christ is in control and will bring about what is best.

11:23 will rise again. The Pharisees and other Jewish groups believed in a general resurrection. She would have understood Jesus' comment as simply an appropriate expression of comfort at a funeral. Other mourners, wishing to comfort her and assure her that they knew Lazarus had been a good man, probably said very similar things to her.

11:25 I am the resurrection and the life. This claim would jar anyone at a funeral! Jesus focuses Martha's attention not on the doctrine of the general resurrection, but on him as the source of that resurrection. **even if he dies, will live.** Spiritual life that will not end at physical death is in view here. In this verse and in verse 26, Jesus is asserting his sovereign power over death and his ability to give life.

11:26 Do you believe this? Jesus directly confronts Martha with this claim. Does she see him only as a healer or as the Lord of life? Jesus on several occasions made a point of giving his followers an opportunity to declare where they stood in relationship to him. A similar instance is when he asked Peter, "But you ..., who do you say I am?" (Matt. 16:15).

11:27 In this verse, Martha declares by means of four terms exactly who Jesus is. **Lord.** This can mean simply "sir," a polite form of address. Whereas in verse 21 it may have that intent, in this verse the author probably is using it in the sense of a title for deity since

the rest of Martha's statement is full of spiritual insight into his identity. **Messiah, the Son of God, who was to come into the world.** In calling him the Christ, Martha acknowledges Jesus as the One who delivers and saves his people from the power of sin and death. Her recognition of him as the Son of God shows her insight into his divine identity. The meaning behind this title is that he is God, sharing the Father's essential nature just as a child shares the characteristics of his or her parents. It was this claim to be the Son of God that was the real grounds for the opposition against him. The final phrase, "who was to come into the world," refers to the expectation that one day a leader like Moses would arise (Deut. 18:18). This too acknowledges his authority and divine commission.

11:32 Mary. That Mary stayed at home when Jesus came (v. 20) seems to have been an indication of despair, for otherwise the one who had shown so much devotion to Christ in other situations (v. 2; Luke 10:38–42) would certainly have come to him right away for comfort.

11:39 he already stinks. Even if Martha knew of the others Jesus had raised (Matt. 11:5; Mark 5:22–43; Luke 7:11–15), they were people who had been dead for only a short time. By the fourth day the actual decomposition of the body had begun and therefore no resuscitation could be possible.

11:40 Didn't I tell you. This may be a reference to the message in verse 4, or the implication of what he meant by his declaration to Martha in verse 25. The sign miracles in this gospel have consistently been regarded as demonstrations of Jesus' identity. They reveal his glory (2:11) and, based on them, people make decisions about who he is (6:14; 9:32–33). This final sign will reveal what has been alluded to all along—Jesus is God.

11:44 bound hand and foot with linen strips. While burial customs included wrapping the body with cloth and spices (19:40), this was not intended to preserve the body, like the ancient Egyptian process of mummification, but only as a sign of honor for the deceased person.

[1]Corrie ten Boom with John and Elizabeth Sherril, *The Hiding Place* (Chappaqua, NY: Chosen Books, Inc., 1971), p. 202.

Session 8

JOY FOR THE JOURNEY

Scripture Luke 24:13–43

 ## LAST WEEK

In last week's session, we saw how God can bring us blessings and remind us of his love, even during extremely difficult circumstances. We heard the inspiring stories of the "bottomless" vitamin bottle and the raising of Lazarus from the dead, and were encouraged to look for blessings among the trials of our own life. This week we will focus on the joy God wants us to have along our journey of faith as we see how grief is transformed into joy for a young woman with multiple sclerosis and the two disciples on the road to Emmaus.

 ## Ice-Breaker : 15 min.
CONNECT WITH YOUR GROUP

Leader

Make sure any visitors feel welcome, and then begin this final session with a word of prayer and thanksgiving for this time together. Choose one or two Ice-Breaker questions to discuss.

We are in the "pursuit of happiness." Before we go on to consider the source of deepest joy, take turns sharing your responses to the following questions.

1. What is the greatest distance you have walked? Were you in shape for it or were you worn out at the end?

2. Have you ever met someone you really should have recognized and not had a clue who it was? What happened?

3. If you were traveling and a stranger in the next seat struck up a conversation, how would you be likely to respond?
   ○ Make some polite rejoinder and go back to my book.
   ○ Keep a lively conversation going until the plane lands.
   ○ Get out my pillow and begin to snore pointedly.
   ○ Ask the attendant to change my seat.
   ○ I always eat a lot of garlic before I travel so this won't happen.
   ○ Try to share the Gospel with the person.

Study Time: 30 min.
READ ÷ DISCUSS

Leader
Select two members of the group ahead of time to read aloud the Life Story and the Scripture passage. Then discuss the Questions for Interaction, dividing into subgroups as necessary.

LIFE STORY ILLUSTRATION

Joy Beyond Circumstances

This is the true story of a woman of great faith. She was not famous, except to her circle of family and friends; she never wrote a book or spoke at a conference or traveled as a missionary to a foreign land. But she was one who walked with Christ. She passed through sorrow and suffering to unspeakable joy on the other side. Her Lord has wiped away all her tears now, for her the pain is over and the glory begun; for those she left behind, the same Lord who comforted her is close and her shining testimony is not forgotten.

Debbie was still a young woman when she discovered that she had multiple sclerosis. Her youngest child was only four, her oldest barely a teenager. Sometimes people can live for a long time with MS with minimal discomfort, but not in Debbie's case. Her body degenerated quickly, and it was not long before she was confined to a wheelchair, and then to her bed.

At first, she begged God to heal her. Her children were still young, they needed her. And her dear husband—she loved him so. Surely it would be God's will to heal her.

But he said, "No."

Then she prayed to die. What good could it do for her to stay alive, confined to bed, a burden for everyone? Surely God would end the suffering and take her home quickly.

But he said, "No."

"All right then," she said. "If you won't take me and you won't heal me, use me!"

And he said, "Pray." So Debbie began to pray. She had nothing else to do, so she prayed for her children and her husband. She prayed for her friends and for every need that she heard about. She grew closer and closer to God. After all, you can't talk with a person constantly without getting to know him better. God's love shone in her, and her friends stopped in often to do what they could to help her. It hurt to see her physical condition, but they loved her and they loved the Christ they saw in her. Sometimes she still wept in frustration at her own helplessness, in sorrow for her family. Her friends saw this too, but deeper than all the physical problems was the joy. One week as a friend was visiting, Debbie turned to her and said, "I would not trade my knowledge of the Lord for health."

As time went on, she could hardly speak at all any more, but she could still pray. She lay in her bed, unable to even scratch her own nose, her beautiful red hair pulled up in a ponytail to keep it out of the way. Her father telephoned one day just to see how she was doing. Speech was hard, so Debbie's response was brief. "Physically, no," she said. "Spiritually, yes."

Debbie had found true joy; not based on health or wealth or beauty; not based on her temperament, her achievements or what she deserved; not based on where she was but on the One who was with her.

SCRIPTURE PASSAGE

Joy for the journey comes from only one source. Sometimes it comes hand in hand with sorrow, sometimes with beauty, but always it comes when we are walking close to the Lord. He is the source of real joy. Read Luke 24:13–43 and see what brought joy to the disciples after the sorrow and desolation they felt at the time of the Crucifixion. This passage takes place on the same day that the women saw the empty tomb.

On the Road to Emmaus

13Now that same day two of them were on their way to a village called Emmaus, which was about seven miles from Jerusalem. 14Together they were discussing everything that had taken place. 15And while they were discussing and arguing, Jesus Himself came near and began to walk along with them. 16But they were prevented from recognizing Him. 17Then He asked them, "What is this dispute that you're having with each other as you are walking?" And they stopped walking and looked discouraged.

18The one named Cleopas answered Him, "Are You the only visitor in Jerusalem who doesn't know the things that happened there in these days?"

19"What things?" He asked them.

So they said to Him, "The things concerning Jesus the Nazarene, who was a Prophet powerful in action and speech before God and all the people, 20and how our chief priests and leaders handed Him over to be sentenced to death, and they crucified Him. 21But we were hoping that He was the One who was about to redeem Israel. Besides all this, it's the third day since these things happened. 22Moreover, some women from our group astounded us. They arrived early at the tomb, 23and when they didn't find His body, they came and reported that they had seen a vision of angels who said He was alive. 24Some of those who were with us went to the tomb and found it just as the women had said, but they didn't see Him."

25He said to them, "How unwise and slow you are to believe in your hearts all that the prophets have spoken! 26Didn't the Messiah have to suffer these things and enter into His glory?" 27Then beginning with Moses and all the Prophets, He interpreted for them in all the Scriptures the things concerning Himself.

28They came near the village where they were going, and He gave the impression that He was going farther. 29But they urged Him: "Stay with us, because it's almost evening, and now the day is almost over." So He went in to stay with them.

30It was as He reclined at the table with them that He took the bread, blessed and broke it, and gave it to them. 31Then their eyes were opened, and they recognized Him; but He disappeared from their sight. 32So they said to each other, "Weren't our hearts ablaze within us while He was talking with us on the road and explaining the Scriptures to us?" 33That very hour they got up and returned to Jerusalem. They found the Eleven and those with them gathered together, 34who said, "The Lord has certainly been raised, and has appeared to Simon!" 35Then they began to describe what had happened on the road, and how He was made known to them in the breaking of the bread.

36And as they were saying these things, He Himself stood among them. He said to them, "Peace to you!" 37But they were startled and terrified and thought they were seeing a ghost. ³⁸"Why are you troubled?" He asked them. "And why do doubts arise in your hearts? ³⁹Look at My hands and My feet, that it is I Myself! Touch Me and see, because a ghost does not have flesh and bones as you can see I have." ⁴⁰Having said this, He showed them His hands and feet. ⁴¹But while they still could not believe for joy, and were amazed, He asked them, "Do you have anything here to eat?" ⁴²So they gave Him a piece of a broiled fish, ⁴³and He took it and ate in their presence.

Luke 24:13–43

 ## QUESTIONS FOR INTERACTION

Leader
Refer to the Summary and Study Notes at the end of this session as needed. If 30 minutes is not enough time to answer all of the questions in this section, conclude the Bible Study by answering question 7.

1. How would you describe your joy level this past week?
   ○ Pretty dismal.
   ○ I felt peace in spite of circum-stances.
   ○ I felt so good I could hardly keep from bouncing off the walls.
   ○ I don't think I know what joy is.

2. How would you define "joy?" What do you think you can do to increase the joy in your life?

3. What is the closest you have come to being in a position like Debbie's in the Life Story we read? How did you handle it?

4. How long has it been since you have "taken a walk" with Jesus and really listened to him? What do you think it would take for you to get into the habit of talking with him more?

5. What does this story of the two disciples on the road to Emmaus remind you of in your own spiritual journey?
   ○ A time when I was feeling hopeless and confused.
   ○ A time when I met God when I least expected it.
   ○ A time when I felt that God really opened my eyes to some spiritual truths.
   ○ A time when I enjoyed the joy of communion with God.
   ○ Other_____.

6. How did Jesus prove that he truly physically rose from the dead, and was not a ghost? What kept the disciples from believing that he was real even though they saw him with their own eyes?

7. Do you find this story hard to believe, or do you find it an encouragement to your faith?

 ## GOING DEEPER:
If your group has time and/or wants a challenge, go on to this question.

---

8. What was the turning point in the spiritual understanding of the two disciples? When have you had a similar turning point in your own spiritual understanding?

 ## Caring Time : 15 min.
APPLY THE LESSON AND PRAY FOR ONE ANOTHER

Leader
Conclude this final Caring Time by praying for each member and asking for God's blessing in any plans to start a new group or to continue to study together.

Gather around each other now in this final time of sharing and prayer. Encourage one another to keep close to God and to remember each of the lessons for the journey that we have studied together.

1. What special joys has God given you over the course of this study?

2. In what way is the knowledge of the bodily resurrection of Christ an encouragement to you?

3. What will you remember the most about this group? How would you like the group to continue to pray for you?

Summary: On the first day of the week, the very same day that the women had found the empty tomb, two disciples were traveling toward the town of Emmaus. They were perplexed and discouraged by the events of the past week. As they talked, Jesus came up and joined their conversation, but, as happened to Mary Magdalene (John 20:14), they were kept from recognizing him. He explained to them from the Scriptures the plan for the Messiah, and showed them that his suffering and death were exactly what they should have expected. Not until Jesus broke bread with them at supper did they realize who he was. When they went to tell the others that they had seen him, he appeared again and calmed their fears by showing them his wounds and eating some fish to show that he was really real.

24:13 two of them. These were not two of the remaining eleven apostles, but two followers of Jesus who lived near Jerusalem. They were probably returning home after the Passover feast. **Emmaus.** The site of this village is uncertain.

24:18 Cleopas. While this man was probably a figure Luke's readers would know, who he is remains uncertain today. **Are you the only visitor in Jerusalem.** The events that occurred— Jesus betrayal, trials and crucifixion—so dominated their minds that they could not comprehend anyone not having heard of them.

24:19 a Prophet. These men had respect for Jesus as a man of God, but after the Crucifixion they seemed reluctant to call him the Messiah.

24:21 to redeem Israel. To free the Jewish nation from bondage to Rome and establish the kingdom of God (1:68; 2:38; 21:28,31; Titus 2:14; 1 Peter 1:18).

24:26 Didn't the Messiah have to suffer. The need for the Messiah to suffer was proclaimed in Isaiah 53. **and enter into His glory.** The messianic glory was a common expectation of the Jews, but his suffering was not.

24:27 Moses and all the Prophets. This was a way of referring to all the Old Testament Scriptures (16:31). Jesus claims that all the Old Testament teachings about the Servant of the Lord, the Son of Man, the Son of David and the Messiah apply to him. It is these teachings taken collectively that explain who he is and what he came to do.

24:30 took the bread, blessed and broke it. While this is a simple enough description of how a meal would begin, it is probably meant to carry overtones of the Lord's Supper (22:19).

PERSONAL NOTES

PERSONAL NOTES

PERSONAL NOTES

PERSONAL NOTES